A catalogue record for this book is available from the Argentinean Library
ISBN 987-96999-2-0

Front cover composition by Monika Schillat and OFFSET NIS
Illustrations by Monika Schillat
Text copyright © Monika Schillat 2002
Illustration copyright © Monika Schillat 2002

Schillat, Monika, Antarctic Bestiary, Ushuaia, Fuegia, 2002
ISBN 987-96999-2-0

© 2002, Monika Schillat
Hecho el depósito que dispone la ley 11.723
Impreso en Argentina

Antarctic Bestiary

Monika Schillat

Editorial Fuegia, Ushuaia 2002

To my brother and sister,
Arno and Sonja,
not only siblings but great friends.

Prologue

edieval bestiaries depicted strange and mysterious creatures, allegories from distant new lands filled with wonders. In countless illuminated manuscripts from the Romanesque and Gothic periods, animals, both real and fantastic, make their appearances.

The bestiarium became one of the most important genres of medieval secular manuscripts. Often the beast depicted would be assigned a characteristic that

accorded with human behavior or personality traits; the bee would be described as the paradigm of the model citizen, the beaver as an industrious villager. Such classifications foreshadowed the popularity of the encyclopedias of the Middle Ages and the more scientific compilations of the Enlightenment.

Books in medieval times bestowed a certain standing upon their owners, and illuminated books, in particular, represented wealth and power. Throughout their history, illuminated books must have been appreciated as works of art, and certainly in the Renaissance they were commissioned and collected as such.

Monks in cloisters, bowed over books, pens in hand, were busy illuminating the collections for people to learn about strange beasts and other wonderful things. First of all, the materials - vellum and parchment, ink, coloured pigments, powdered gold and gold leaf - would be prepared and gathered together. The vellum and parchment, from calf or sheep skin, was laboriously prepared: soaked in water and lime, then scraped and stretched. Once dried, the vellum was folded into halves, quarters or eights, depending on the required size of the book. These pages would then be trimmed and stitched together. Ink was made from powdered carbon - soot or lamp-black or irongall - which was kept in a cow horn, and materials for the coloured pigments came from a variety of animal, vegetable and mineral sources.

Once the materials had been gathered and prepared, the paper marked, and the illuminator had indicated the spaces needed for the decorated borders, initial letters and miniatures, the scribe could begin work. With a pen in one hand and a curved knife in the other, the latter being used for sharpening the pen and scraping out mistakes.

And there are still scribes and illuminators among us. Even the techniques of illumination used today are very similar to those used in medieval times. Today we would like to present a modern book, full of extraordinary designs for initials and miniatures inspired by different styles, such as Celtic, Romanesque and Gothic. The author – imagening what would have happened if a group of medieval monks and scholars had reached the White Continent – presents us with a wonderful collection of stories about antarctic animals.

Monika Schillat's recent work takes its cue from the ancient compendia of knowledge. Part historian and visual alchemist, she simulates in delicate ink and watercolour sketches a medieval Antarctic bestiary. Thereby she conjures up inner thoughts, codification of human as well as animal habits and symbols of emotional states. Penguins are addicted to music. They play the harp and listen to the lute. A leopard seal becomes a metaphor of terror. The snowy sheathbill may be understood as an emblem of peace and hope. But fun also plays a key role in this beastly gathering. Sirenes and dragons are part of the animals living in the medieval Antarctic. The result is both beautiful and amusing.

Graciela Ramacciotti

Opposite to the northern
or arctic pole lies the
ntarctic.
And, as the northern
hemisphere lies under
the constellation of
Arktos the Bear, so Aristotle told us the
unknown land to the south must be Antarktikos,
or the total opposite, the Polus Antarcticus.

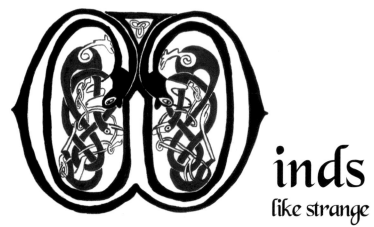inds
like strange

beasts fight in the heavans of Antarctica

hese westerlies give birth to great
storms that haunt us.

Polus Antarcticus

nd out of whose womb came this ice? And the hoary frost of heaven, who hath gendered it? The waters are hid as with a stone, and the face of the deep is frozen.

Job 38, 29

They that go down to the sea in ships, that do business in great waters, these see the works of the Lord, and his wonders in the deep.

Psalm 107:23-24

 **ollymawk** is the name seafarers gave to a bird of wondrous size

Beyond the torrid zone and the margin of the habitable world, there exists a bird of great size, whose wings together are wider than a well-built man is tall. It is thought to fly further and more continuously than any known bird, needing neither continent nor islands to rest its wings. For food it plucks large fishes from the deep and even with vice-like grip can lift a man from the deck of his vessel. By sailors it is feared as being the harbinger of ill fortune and the cause of mighty tempests.

Dragon is most greatest of all serpents,

and oft he is drawn out of his den, and riseth up into the air, and the air is moved by him, and also the sea swelleth against his venom, and he hath a crest with a little mouth, and draweth breath at small pipes and straight, and reareth his tongue, and hath teeth like a saw, and hath strength, and not only in teeth, but also in his tail, arid grieveth both with biting and with stinging, and hath not so much venom as other serpents: For to the end to slay anything, to him venom is not needful, for whom he findeth he slayeth.

The cause why the dragon desireth blood, is coldness of the blood, by the which the dragon desireth to cool himself. The dragon is a full thirsty beast, insomuch that unless he may have water enough to quench his great thirst; and openeth his mouth therefore against the wind, to quench the burning of his thirst in that wise. Therefore when he seeth ships sail in the sea in great wind, he flieth against the sail to take their cold wind, and overthroweth the ship sometimes for greatness of body. And when the ship men see the dragon come nigh, and know his coming by the water that swelleth ayenge him, they strike the sail anon, and scape in that wise.

irene sicut dicit phisiologus mortifera animalia sunt.

Sirenes are sea beasts wonderly shapen. The mermaid draweth shipmen to peril by sweetness of song. It is said, that sirens are serpents with crests. And some men say, that they are fishes of the sea in likeness of women. Some men feign that there are three Sirens some-deal maidens, and some-deal fowls with claws and wings, and one of them singeth with voice, and another with a pipe, and the third with an harp, and they please so shipmen, with likeness of song, that they draw them to peril and to shipbreach, but the truth is, that they were strong whores, that drew men that passed by them to poverty and to mischief. And Physiologus saith it is a beast of the sea, wonderly shapen as a maid from the navel upward and a fish from the navel downward, and this wonderful beast is glad and merry in tempest, and sad and heavy in fair weather.

With sweetness of song this beast maketh ship-men to sleep, and when she seeth that they are asleep, she goeth into the ship, and ravisheth which she may take with her, and bringeth him into a dry place, and maketh him first lie by her, and if he will not or may not, then she slayeth him and eateth his flesh.

 he sea
bear liveth
most long, and that is known by working and
wasting of his teeth.

Some sea bears be short with crisp
hair and mane, these seals fight not; and some
sea bears have simple hair of mane, and those
seals have sharp and fierce hearts, and by their
foreheads their virtue is known in the beast,
and their stedfastness in the head; and when
they be beset with hunters, then they behold the
earth, for to dread the less the hunters and their
gins, that them have beset about.

Some
sea ·
bears
be · ..

short with ·
crisp hair ·
and mane · ..

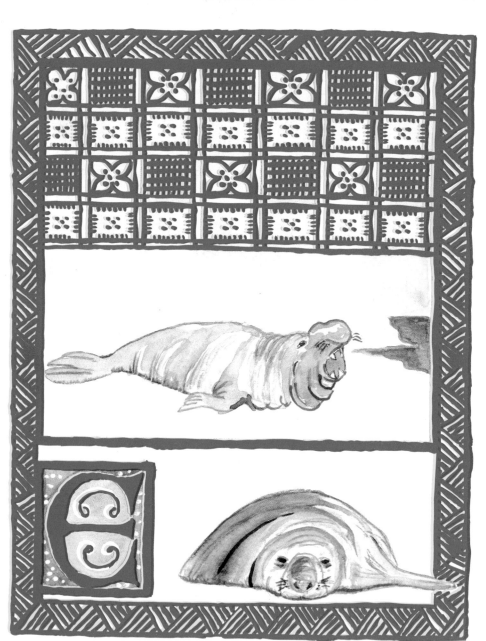

The southern elephant seal is a most wondrous sea creature. It feeds on squid and fish. Bull elephants seals weigh up to 4 tonnes. The cows in his harem are one eighth of this size. Bulls have a big nose with wrinkles like an elephant's trunk.

Leopard seal is a beast most cruel, and is gendered in spouse-breach of a serpent and of a lioness, and pursueth his prey startling and leaping under the water and not running, and if he taketh not his prey in the third leap, or in the fourth, then he stinteth for indignation, and goeth backward as though he were overcome.

He sleeps on the ice alone. Leopard seal is an evil beast, when he eateth, and resteth much when he hath no hunger: he is full hardy, and loveth well to play with a penguin, if he may take him and slyeth him afterward, and eateth him at the last. I have read in a book that a string made of a leopard seal's gut, put among harp strings made of the guts of sheep, destroyeth and corrupteth them, as the eagle's feathers put among culvours', pulleth and gnaweth them, if they be there left together long in one place.

n South Georgia and close to the Shag Rocks, we found huge Mackarel icefish. They can grow to over half a metre in length and eat the little krill.

The schrimp, **K**rill is the most important of the creatures name: Euphasia superbia

Balena
autem
sunt inmense magnitudinis bestie

n monday morning, when we were unloading the ship we saw a tall black triangle coming at us. It was a huge dorsal fin of a most wondrous creature. A little later Killer whales were all around us. They are as dangerous as wolves and hunt the little penguins as well as young sea bears and even huge whales. Our sailors felt most insecure in the presence of these big, black hunters.

 iggest among the fish is the w h a l e . The name whalefish comes from the Anglo Saxon word hwelan, to roar, to bellow, from the noise they make in blowing.

 elphines certum habent nomen propie

nowy Sheath.
bi.
ll.

olumba simplex avus
est, fello caret et osculo
amorem concitat.
Ita predicatores carent ira. Et
magnitudine quia licet irascantur
tum non dicitur ira cum

rationabiliter irascantur. Habent
gemitum pro cantu. Ita predicatores
procul a moto cantu et amore
seculi geminit pro suis et aliorum
peccatis. Nec facerat rostro
et hoc bonum competit.

 orvus sive corax nomen

a sone gutturis habet quod voce corracinet

Penguins
are a strange
sort of beasts.

e found a strange species of goose, some of us thought they were a mixture of beast, bird and fish for they could not fly. We called them penguins. They walk upright like men and shake their heads in a strange way. We took plenty of these strange fowl and salted their meat for the sailors. Their flesh was quite tasty to the hungry men. We also took their eggs, which we painted with oil and put into caskets full of sand where they stayed fresh for months.

uring the last few days we saw many of the great penguins, and several were caught and brought on board alive. They are remarkably stupid, they are not afraid of us and sometimes they leap upon the ice as if to attack us, but without the smallest means of either of offence or defence. Its principle food consists of crustaceous animals. Its capture afforded great amusement to the sailors, for when alarmed and endeavouring to escape, it makes its way over deep snow faster than they could follow it by lying down on its belly and impelling itself by its powerful feet, it slides along upon the surface of the snow at a great pace, steadying itself by extending its finlike wings which alternately touch the ground on the side opposite to the propelling leg.

ockhopper penguins have a black head and back and a snowy-white front. Flaring out from the side of its head, above its eyes, are tufted wings of yellow plumes. The penguin's bill is red, strong and deadly sharp.

The stench at the nesting site is very strong, the yelling of the strange animals most annoying and discordant. The nests are placed so thickly that you cannot help treading on eggs at almost every step. A parent bird sits on each nest with its sharp beak erect and open, ready to bite, yelling savagely "caa, caa, urr, urr", its red eyes gleaming in its plumes at half-cock, quivering with rage.

The sea coast was replete with an oceanic bird, that we had not seen before. Their wings differ but little from paddles and they cannot fly. We did not know if they had feathers or wool on their bodies for they looked like brown sheep.

Acknowledgements

The final stages in the production of any book are very important and I was very fortunate to have my good friend Graciela Ramacciotti designing this one together with the very talented Carlos Gabriel Pinto. Graciela is also the book's editor and never lost faith in the project. Thanks from my heart.